W9-BXA-601

SIMPLY SCIENCE

Seasons

by Patricia Ryon Quiri

Content Adviser: Terrence E. Young Jr., M.Ed., M.L.S., Jefferson Parish (La.) Public Schools

Reading Adviser: Dr. Linda D. Labbo, Department of Reading Education, College of Education, The University of Georgia

COMPASS POINT BOOKS
Minneapolis, Minnesota

For my friends and colleagues, Jill Granstrom, Mary Hart, Lisa Kerns, Camille Miller, and Janet Vanderlick

Compass Point Books
3109 West 50th Street, #115
Minneapolis, MN 55410

Visit Compass Point Books on the Internet at *www.compasspointbooks.com* or e-mail your request to *custserv@compasspointbooks.com*

Photographs ©: International Stock/Edmund Nagele, cover; International Stock/Novastock, 4; International Stock/Caroline Wood, 5; ESA/Tsado/Tom Stack and Associates, 6; Visuals Unlimited/Arthur Gurmankin, 7; Unicorn Stock Photos/Jean Higgins, 8; International Stock/Michael Agliolo, 9; International Stock/Richard Pharaoh, 10; Marilyn Moseley LaMantia, 11; International Stock/Mitch Diamond, 12; Visuals Unlimited/D. Cavagnaro, 13; Paul A. Souders/Corbis, 15; Root Resources/Kohout Productions, 16; John Gerlach/Tom Stack and Associates, 17; Victor Englebert, 19; Marilyn Moseley LaMantia, 20; International Stock/Scott Campbell, 22; Color Box/FPG International, 23; Unicorn Stock Photos/Fred Jordan, 24; Visuals Unlimited/Tom J. Ulrich, 25; Telegraph Colour Library/FPG International, 26; International Stock/Joe Willis, 27; Photo Network/T.J. Florian, 28; Unicorn Stock Photos/Jeff Greenberg, 29.

Editors: E. Russell Primm, Emily J. Dolbear, and Melissa Stewart
Photo Researcher: Svetlana Zhurkina
Photo Selector: Dawn Friedman
Design: Bradfordesign, Inc.

Library of Congress Cataloging-in-Publication Data
Quiri, Patricia Ryon.
Seasons / by Patricia Ryon Quiri.
p. cm. — (Simply science)
Includes bibliographical references (p.) and index.
Summary: Briefly describes why we have seasons and how they affect people and other living things.
ISBN 0-7565-0034-6 (hardcover : lib. bdg.)
1. Seasons—Juvenile literature. [1. Seasons.] I. Title. II. Simply science (Minneapolis, Minn.)
QB637.4 .Q5 2000
508.2—dc21 00-008578

Printed in the United States of America.

Table of Contents

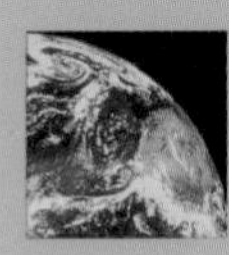

The Four Seasons

Do you have a favorite **season**? Many people like spring most of all. Other people like summer, autumn, or winter best. In most parts of the world, the air temperature and the weather change. In North America, summer is hotter than winter and spring is a time for new life. Fall is a time to get ready for the cold winter ahead.

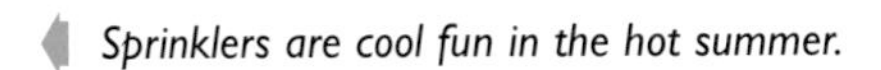

Sprinklers are cool fun in the hot summer.

Sledding is fun in the snowy winter.

Earth Orbits and Spins

Think of Earth as a big ball that **orbits**, or moves around, the Sun. It takes Earth about 365 days, or one **year**, to make a full orbit. This means that between your last birthday and your next birthday, Earth will make one trip around the Sun.

Earth seen from space

Earth's orbit around the sun

As Earth orbits the Sun, it also spins. Look at a globe that shows how Earth is shaped. Place one pin at the North Pole and another pin at the South Pole. Earth

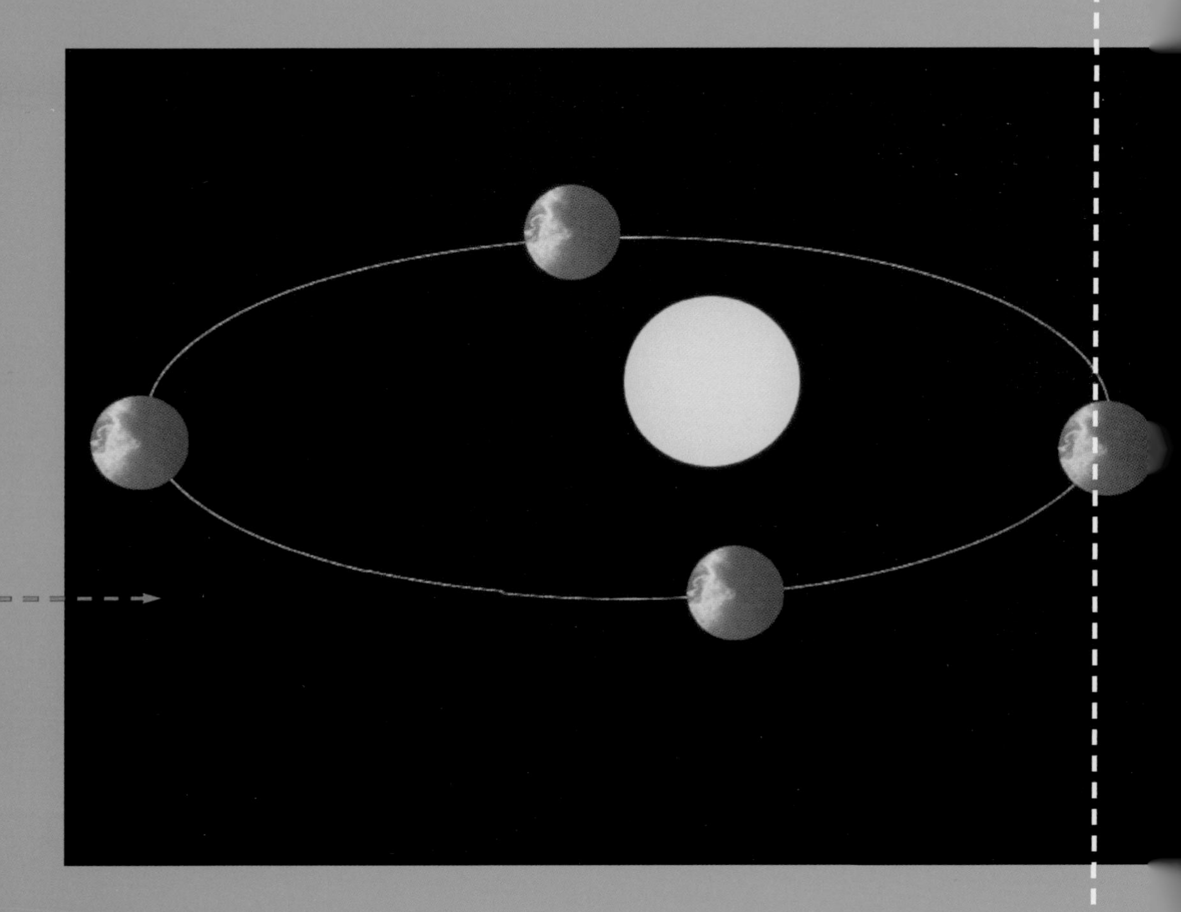

spins on an **imaginary** line that runs between the two pins. This imaginary line is called the **axis**. It runs through the center of Earth.

As Earth spins, different parts of the world face the Sun. It is daytime in the parts of the world facing the Sun. That is why daytime is bright and sunny. It is night in places that are not facing the Sun. That is why it is dark outside at night. It takes about twenty-four hours, or one **day**, for Earth to spin one time.

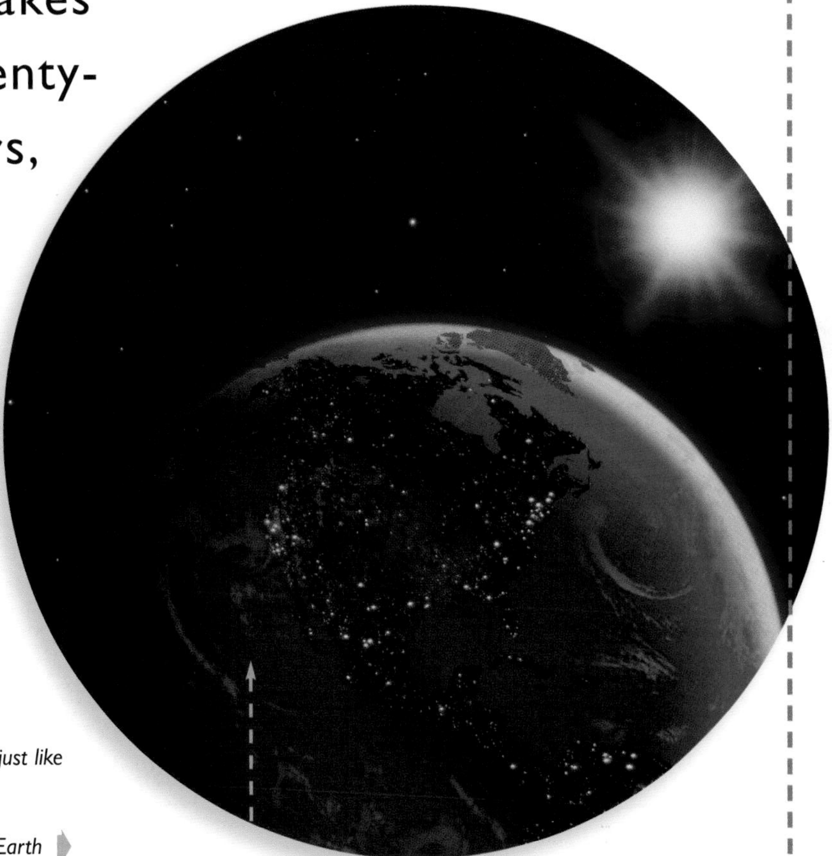

A globe spins on its axis just like Earth does.

It is night on the side of Earth that faces away from the sun.

What Causes the Seasons?

Earth moves very slowly, so we do not feel Earth spinning on its **axis** or orbiting around the Sun. We know Earth spins because sometimes it is day, and sometimes it is night. We know Earth orbits because the seasons change.

The **equator** is an imaginary line that goes around the middle of Earth. The part of the world north of the equator is called the Northern Hemisphere.

When the North Pole is tipped toward the Sun, the rays of the Sun are

The equator is marked in red on this map.

It is summer in the Northern Hemisphere.

very strong and very direct in the Northern Hemisphere. It is summer for people in North America, Europe, and most of Asia.

When the North Pole is tipped away from the Sun, it is winter in the Northern Hemisphere. The Sun's rays are not strong and they are not direct.

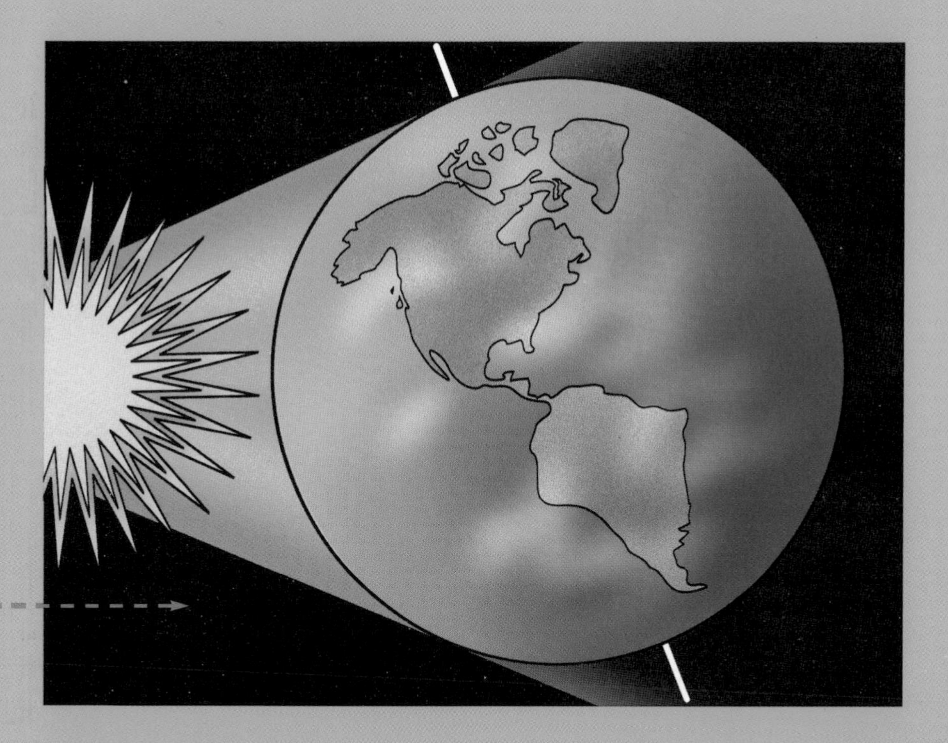

The Start of Summer

Have you ever noticed that during the summer, you can play outside longer? There are more daylight hours and fewer hours of darkness during the summer.

Summer begins on the day when the Sun is at its highest point in the sky.

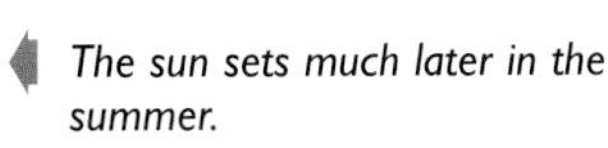

The sun sets much later in the summer.

Picking summer vegetables

In North America, summer usually begins around June 21. Because the Sun is so high in the sky, it takes a long time to move from where it starts out at sunrise to where it ends up at sunset. That is why the first day of summer is the longest day of the year.

For people who live in the Southern Hemisphere, however, summer begins on December 21. The seasons are opposite there. When the North Pole tips toward the Sun, the South Pole tips away from the Sun.

Children in New Zealand can wear shorts in February!

Winter Begins

During the winter, it gets darker earlier and you can't play outside after dinner. We have more hours of darkness and fewer hours of sunlight.

In the Northern Hemisphere, the shortest day of the year is around December 21. The Sun is at its lowest point in the

Night comes earlier in the winter.

An early sunset in the winter woods

sky on that day. It takes a much shorter time for the Sun to travel across the sky on the first day of winter than on the first day of summer.

For people who live in the Southern Hemisphere, winter begins on June 21. That is when the South Pole is tipped away from the Sun.

Winter in South America

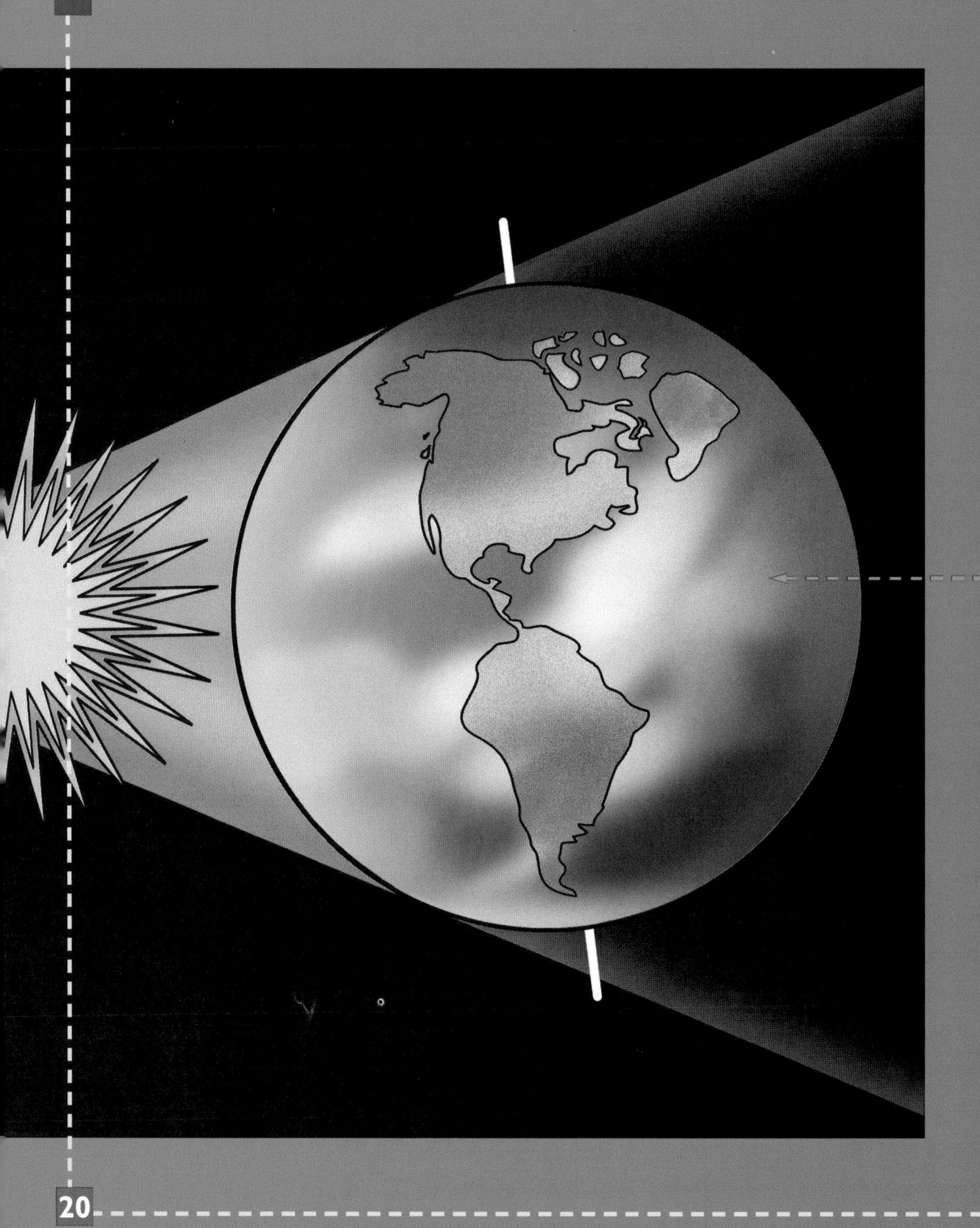

The Middle Seasons

During spring and autumn, the Sun is at a middle point in the sky. Earth is tipped only a little. Daylight hours and nighttime hours are about the same.

In the Northern Hemisphere, spring begins around March 21. Autumn begins around September 23. On these days, Earth is not tipped at all. There are about twelve hours of daytime light and twelve hours of nighttime darkness.

It is spring and autumn on Earth because Earth is tipped only a little.

Spring and Autumn

In spring, the air warms up and the ground begins to thaw. Plants sprout new leaves and flowers begin to bloom. Many birds return from their warmer winter homes and begin to build nests. Some other animals wake up from their winter sleep. Spring is a time of new life.

A farmer in a field of new crops

New buds and flowers on a tree in spring

In some parts of North America, autumn is a colorful time of year. The leaves of many trees turn orange, red, or yellow. Then the leaves fall to the ground. Some birds and insects begin a long journey to a warmer place. Other animals grow a thick, warm coat and curl up in a cozy burrow. Still others are active all winter. They gather plenty of food to eat during the long, cold winter.

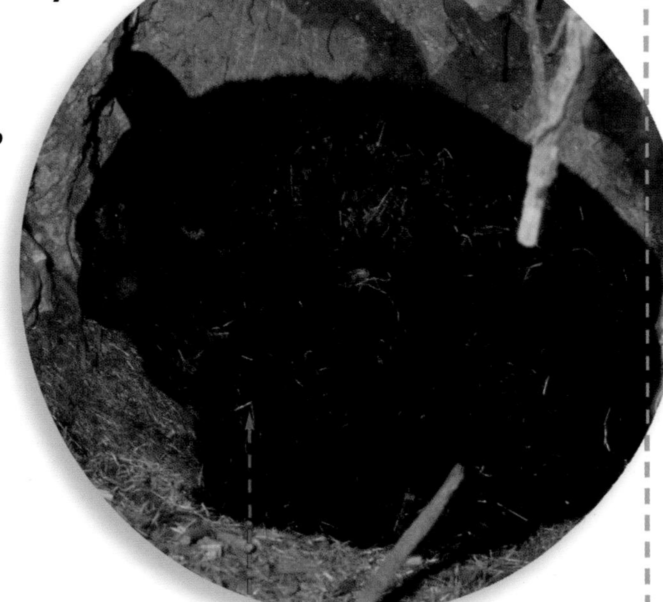

Maple trees turn beautiful colors in autumn.

A black bear spends the winter sleeping, or hibernating, in a cave.

Living Season by Season

In North America, each season has different weather. The changes in weather affect our lives. In summer, you probably wear shorts and a T-shirt. You may spend your time swimming or playing baseball. In winter, you probably wear long

A summer day at the beach

Coming home from a baseball game

pants, sweaters, sweatshirts, and jackets to stay warm. If you live in a place that gets snow, you can sled, or ski, or build a snowman.

Have you decided what your favorite season is? Maybe you like all the different times of the year. Now that you know about spring, summer, autumn, and winter, go out and enjoy each day of each season!

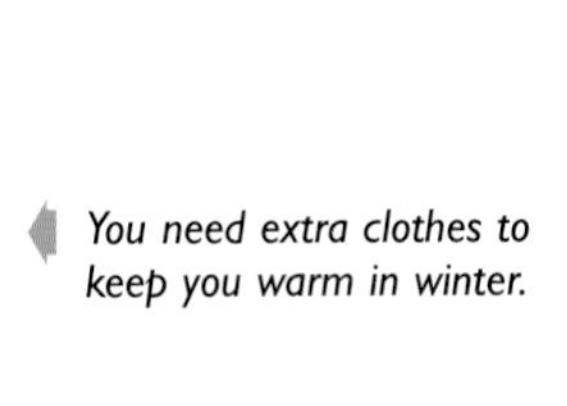

You need extra clothes to keep you warm in winter.

Sledding in the snow

Glossary

axis—an imaginary line that goes from the North Pole, through the center of Earth, down to the South Pole

day—the time it takes Earth to spin once on its axis—twenty-four hours

equator—the imaginary line that goes around the middle of the Earth, separating north from south

imaginary—not real

orbits—moves around

season—one of the four time periods that make up a year

year—the time it takes Earth to orbit the Sun one time—about 365 days

Did You Know?

- In North America, each season is about three months long.
- Some parts of the world have just two seasons—a wet season and a dry season.
- In ancient times, people had all kinds of ways of measuring the seasons. It was important to know when spring would start, so that farmers could plant their crops at the right time.

Want to Know More?

At the Library

Arnosky, Jim. *Crinkleroot's Nature Almanac.* New York: Simon & Schuster Books for Young Readers, 1999.

Maestro, Betsy. *Why Do Leaves Change Color?* New York: Harper Collins, 1994.

Sipiera, Paul P., and Diane M. *Seasons.* Danbury, Conn.: Children's Press, 1998.

Supraner, Robyn. *I Can Read About Seasons.* Mahwah, N.J.: Troll Communications, 1999.

On the Web

For more information on this topic, use FactHound.

1. Go to *www.facthound.com*
2. Type in this book ID: 0756500346
3. Click on the *Fetch It* button.

FactHound will find the best Web sites for you.

Through the Mail

Farmers' Almanac Order Desk

P.O. Box 1609

Mt. Hope Avenue

Lewiston, ME 04241

To get a copy of this seasonal guide with long-range weather forecasts

On the Road

Fall Foliage in New England

http://www.7almanac.com/articles/fall.html

To find out when the autumn leaves are most beautiful in New England

Index

About the Author

Patricia Ryon Quiri is a graduate of Alfred University and has a bachelor's degree in elementary education. She teaches second grade in the Pinellas County school system and has written twenty-one children's books. Patricia Ryon Quiri lives with her husband, Bob, and their three sons in Palm Harbor, Florida.